The Thing that
Heals

my first year of poems

by Nate Crew

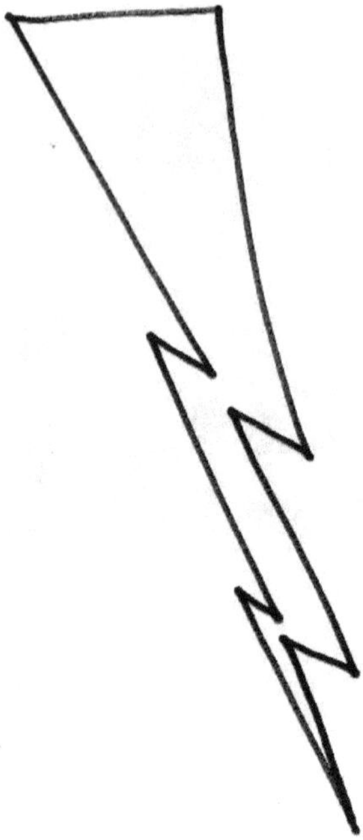

CONTENTS

2

BOOK 1

VERSES FROM THE VALLEY OF DEATH

March 2021

TO STOP AND EXAMINE

Examine these wanderings here on a page
I hanker for silence, so how come these raves?
I'm living by rules that my fingers can tally
Yet where did I get them? An infinite valley

The silently singing complexities there
My lot in them simple and lighter than air
While roaming a landscape, I stop and examine
Where I see a feast when the world sees a famine

The raves are a mistress, the rules are a wife
Be careful to live on the edge of a knife
To pause and to think, and then go without thinking
And go yet again and not drown in your drinking

We favored the simple, the muscular facts
Effectively brutal, full mags and brass tacks
A parachute jump, a new woman's enjoyment
A chest full of metal, a thrilling employment

We raged in the valley, pursuing our prey
Then gaped at the sky of a quiet new day
The thrill of a dangerous life not denying
The blindness of killing, the mystery of dying

A blindness so vile, let me open my eyes
But give me the mystery, where do we rise?
Our thrills undeniable, danger and power
They make us and break us, they heal and devour

A wolfpack of lunatic kings in new lands
Yet pawns in a halfhearted castle of sand
Not missing the babble and bustle and hoarding
Consuming banality we were rewarding

A houseful of trinkets, not stopping to think
At home in a bed where we don't sleep a wink
The honor was real, but the duty suspicious
The cause a bit vague but the power delicious

The trinkets a famine, the valley a feast
The wolf is the most and the pack is the least
The mistress is death when I'm married to living
The future I'm taking, the past I'm forgiving

To dig for an answer, I open a mine

My raves are the shovels, I'm racing with time

I stop and examine, the lower I creep

Don't think I can possibly dig it too deep

FOREVER ANEW

Forever a new revolution arriving
Emerging, revolving
Converging, arising
New mission departing, returning, reviving
Even millennia creeping on slowly
Were only a pause in the furious cavorting
Delighting, highlighting while holding a note
Turning a color in mist, then resuming
The waterfall starting again and again
"New reason, new madness, recurring new birth,"
a fleshy red gene in my fibers is whispering
Pains me with shuddering changing and shifting
Shows me her naked new vision peripheral
Relentlessly bare, not ashamed nor ephemeral
Out on the edge of my sight she is glowing
Quantum connection of everything real
Endlessly raising the bar when it's lowering
Endless new height and new depth, farther reaching
New measures of measureless knowledge inventing
New memory of future beginnings and ends
A present both giving and taking and making
Among us a coming and going and growing

Earning and paying and sharing unraveling

Weaving then leaving a tapestry bold

Loop threading immortal, recurring and terminal

Locus of each new rotation appearing

My nation the crux of a sunrise still dawning

Restoring a sun showing everything new

Reborn as a new generation defiant

Revive a gazelle in the roar of a lion

The blood of our past on a roaring new path

Our peace neither static nor stable nor mild

Our calm never flaccidly feeble, but wild

A gripping acceptance of daybreak eternal

Accept the chaotic red menacing clouds

My gene in a pool now dissolving and raining

Ocean wave surging, expanding and crashing

Embrace an illusion but join the effusion

Everlasting infinite mosaic is shuffling

Beyond you, above you, it flows from within you

Not stopping nor staying, audaciously straying

All turning and burning and furiously churning

An urging emergent

Arriving abundant

Forever emerging

Forever anew

THE THING THAT HEALS

My generation has an agitated question
Yet words will not contain it
This mortal brain cannot obtain a real solution
Let mind eternal gain it

       Let spirit of the earth beneath our feet
       Come pour out through my lines into our
       streets

The parents silently began to hope for meaning
Grandchildren cast about now
Their mindless rushing and anxiety, their pleading
But soil-voice may come out now

       My eyelids shut, kaleidoscopic trance
       I open out to you a cosmic dance

How will you balance if you won't allow both sides?
Receive both pride and meekness
Both love and lust, both light and dark, both left and
right
Both poetry and reason

       Both ego and where it evaporates
       Together may they open out your gates

May lines go here and there, from measured rhyme and rhythm

To chaos and creation

No built foundation, but the roots bring life within them

May each renew the nation

> Await what more the forest will reveal
>
> Awake while I create the thing that heals

FROM THE LUMBEE RIVER TO ME

Come in, paddler, come onto me
Bring in my swirl your new energy
>Sleek curve, you slip long on my fluid
>Skim along my topside
>Rhythmic dip of your paddles, a flowing black stream

We've waited for you, the waters and me

Our soil, paddler, she waited too
Thirsty for me and hungry for you
>Your hardness on her twisting surface
>Yellow butterflies there
>Sandy clay of her taproots enjoying my milk

And craving your sweat, she's longing for you

Touch me, paddler, sweep out your hand
Fingers that plant your seed in our land
>I crave you as she does, your gazing
>Swifter goddess, I am
>Countless seasons awaiting my day in your light

A thirst for my curves you will never withstand

Come in, paddler, stranger to here

Welcome to me as native and near

      Inviting you, follow me, hear me

      See the life-force beneath

      From the greenness above to invisible depth

The writhing and heart you will not see or hear

Sense me, paddler, smell of my mist

Taste me and feel the skin of my hips

      We drive on by the warm rain of summer

      Feel the haze on the fields

      In a county of scot-free invincible souls

The dew of the morning bestowed from my lips

COME OUT WITH ME

Come out with me, you spirited girl
We'll find a truth and go for a whirl
We'll shine a light where nobody knows
We'll beat a path where nobody goes
If not at first, then maybe at last
The light will show a leveler path
Maybe our friends will go with us too
Together move forward
And love what is true

HERE IN MY WORKSPACE,
LOW-HANGING FRUIT

Off with the rhyme, out with the cadence
Now comes the chaos uncontained
Here is the blooming creation

Nearby the marshes,
      I was looking up at scarlet peaches
      at the top of the tree
      out of reach of my hand
To look always silently is good
Yet never silencing the better, the nearer
Nearest to each face
Unfathomed wellspring whose being I never gripped
In front of my eyes, the object hanging lower
Behind them, my workspace

Invisible hand, pulling strands from my tongue
Divine strings, brilliant light yet mostly crimson
Bloody, throbbing, divine, fertile, strumming
Drawing out, stretch infinite length into emptiness

Pulling steady from deeper, longer, more than I
    imagined was in me
And if so heavy rich from me, yet richer from the
    next person surely

His strand, yours, perhaps of an aroma
        that makes mine seem a brick of manure
        reeking of tumultuous death
But is not death the most throbbing of beauties?
Do I not defend the proud, teeming, rotten end
        of an acorn as it sprouts?

My strand is longer and wilder than needed
        The rain is neither sparse nor withholding
        Though I have only just met the marshy
        muse,
        I know her generosity to me and you
My strand is of death and wide beginnings
        As is yours
When memory dies, the strands remain
And without the manifold strand of each and every,
        latent or unfurled,
An abyss would go unanswered, never split open
        Never breathing chords into the silence

This higher workspace of the soul, this strumming
      yarn, yours or mine

Projection of existence onto an unknown canvas

Canvas of a chasm of the potential

      The not yet actualized

Then in the background, behind my eyes, a
      porcelain-like shine

Twin gods of laughter, joyfully bending and
      plucking, no longer heavy

Lines made of shimmering dimensions unmeasured,
      excluded from comprehension

Bands made of reality our science barely touches

Of what bibles only guessed at

Connecting strands of colors more brilliant than
      purest sunlight

Glints of the brightest yet deepest life-green

Hints of colors our eyes never met

Unknowable words before which

      I am less than nothing

The laughter and delight of the twin creators

      a sunnier sense than anything mortal

Yet somehow, I recognized the two

Up, out from my wellspring, now a daily workspace,
      the physical humid, into the marsh
To look always silently is good
Divine bodies and faces in front of me
The flowing black hair, a sheer sundress in Sinjar
The lust of the flesh, the lust of the eyes, and the
      pride of life
I affirm these to be among the truest beauties of
      earthly nights
The low-hanging fruit is by far,
      of all touchable delicacies,
      deepest in beauty and truth

MORNING REAPER

Mama, Mama, look at me

My soul, creation and destruction

Harmless me, murderous me

      Harmless me, finding calm in a shady cliff

      Harmless me, leaving siblings to find my way

      Murderous me, shaking, shattering foreign worlds

      Murderous, I bury my hate in a desert

            Bury again my blood in California

Brother, brother, follow me

"Be strong, be self-controlled and simple"

Curious we, courageous we

      Curious you, seeking knowledge in every place

      Curious you, even though she would never look

      Courageous you, bear the struggles of other souls

      Courageous, we open our eyes too widely

            Don't look to me!

            I am the morning reaper

Brother, please, come stay with me
Ignore my rules, give back your brightness
Joyous be, effusive be
 Joyous you, a bridegroom in his glory
 Joyous you, a man beyond his comrades
 Effusive you, when reaching for the wildness
 Effusive, you examine each perception
  Climbing a live oak forever

Brother, you and I are free
Not harmless, murderous, nor absent
Active we, dynamic we
 Active, you got your knowledge finally
 Active, but you got enough to calm your soul
 Dynamic, I got your presence to shadow me
 Dynamic, yet I sit beneath your oak tree
  Till stepping off,
  we glue the world together

CAROLINA AIR

Of April's virility in Carolina's air
A windy song stolen, taken unaware
From a billion jubilant birds of the past
Yet a solo resounds in my trees unabashed
Arms freshly tanned, extending, stretched out
Face upturned, salute the sun, holler a shout
      Of April's virility in Carolina's air

A windchime rings on the porch openhearted
Aroma borrowed from brothers departed
Shouting their freedom anew in my woods
Wafting their memories, blossoms and buds
Red bird not begrudging me, sharing a tune
Of health and acceptance, of body and bloom
      Young open manhood, full blast and full blare

A fertile bright female peer of mine
Whose body I see this month the first time
Like a robin I whistle my wishing of her
Of mounting and being her transient lover
Or if it's another person I see,

In his or her eyes recognize vibrancy
        He becomes my new brother, I swear

But you there, fractured, sharp and proud
Turned away and refusing my sunny shout
My bloody heart opens to you nonetheless
And I show you a green unfolding dress
Of a tulip tree, where we planted last year
Our drooping losses, watered by tears
        Wishing to bring them back from out there

The wind and her chimes, they breathe in my ear
A familiar voice I faintly hear
Stretching his throat to give me his song
Saying to stretch out my neck before long
To bare my chest and reconcile
To walk with you a lighter mile
        Before we join them all out there

Thundering April cries in my homeland
Window shut in a freeze, now bursting open
A color, a sneeze, eternal youth, hallowed breeze
In wind souls converging, hummingbirds and bees
Peaceably freed of matter and time this spring

Freely drinking life's nectar out there, they sing
Of April's virility in Carolina's air

CATHARTIC WOMAN

Focusing down to a point, cathartic
     (Shooting from there
     Unstoppable prayer)
Condensing reality tight, a target
     (Flowing down here
     Flood open, my dear)
Now pulling your hair as I charge, atomic

The penetration is a rhythm that we know
No understanding when you got to let it go
I drop a hammer and I clamber up a tree
I pick a leaf and you are dropping into me

Why is the verse so bipolar?
     (Rude is my scene
     A jumbled-up dream)
I'm wrestling grabbing your shoulder
     (A holler, a gasp
     A squeal, a laugh)
I push you uphill like a boulder

Raise the heat, hit the beat, drop a sledge
Rocking you high, up with a tide, stop at the ledge

The rock beginning to crumble and melt
I cracked an egg in my spirit, I felt
You wrap your leg and you push and you pull
We're falling free and I'm filling you full

Tumbling down from above, freely spilling
      (An atom dissolved
      Our bodies revolve)
Spinning around in the orbit, fulfilling
      The plowing down here
      Has beaten our fear
Opened the earth on a turf we are tilling

Focusing down to a point, catharsis
      Shooting from there
      Unstoppable prayer
Condensing reality tight, my goddess

BALLAD OF A GENERATION'S UNSUNG HEROES

To each of you that follows
      prime specimens of my species
      crown jewels of civilization
      stalwarts of a new day we may build
The honor of our centuries I give to you
Your dignity is past the horizon
Yet a few words may begin to chase it
I see you each, plain as today's sunrise
      have met or may meet you in my lifetime
      your worth solid as gold

To you, a man of an iron grip
giver of relentless purpose, mover of silent passion
I know you well
To you, woman of an immortal smile
bosom of perfect being, cradle of vibrant life
I revere you

To a daughter's innocent bounty
forever undaunted by dry explanations

To a boy's crisp rudeness
exuberant, defiant, empty of malice

To a magnolia insulted
planted beneath power lines
spreading her shade nonetheless
To a patch of ravished dirt, stripped
burnt, abused, bereaved of her offspring and kin
giving forth new life nonetheless, *mimosa hostilis*

To a savage princess
taking orders from none, going where you feel
burning freedom's torch hotter than any statue
At a campfire by a river, I remember your burn
And to you, a confounded creator
ahead of your times
triumphal vision sure to arrive one day
To the raging bull of a man
relic of bloody fighters in dark bygone ages
reborn a pillar of divine licentious rhythms
To a fading Viking shadow
conqueror behind your times
visceral adventurer at dead ends

To you above all, tomorrow's heroes
the ones earning greatest tribute, ending war for good
who secure aloft the individual soul in eternal peace
your monuments must reach to topple Valhalla

To each of you, apart, alone: accept your laurels
Fill your purpose together with us who see you
Fulfill yourself and pass on your way
        satisfied with our love
and immortal glory will be yours.

GOLDEN PRIVILEGE

A poor boy captured a fly to possess it
    To pluck off its wings
    A privilege of evolution

Grown up, I met a captured man, penniless
Controlled by a warlord "president"
Pressed into an African army from youth
A soldier possessing a wooden amulet
The shaman's threaded charm he cherished
To thwart his rifle from stealing a life
Protect not himself, but those in his sights
Yet I trained him to aim and shoot
And to make his bullets fly true
But before he did it, to hit my target
He handed a friend his wooden amulet
While swatting a fly, I then understood
That in his hand, not a charm of wood
A purity the rich warlord won't control
A silent privilege made of gold

An older boy may finally decide

To let a fly with dignity die

To evolve beyond the lies of old

To see a warlord's riches are fool's gold

And I decline to be dissuaded

From scribbling till I reach his faded village

Of how we each possess his golden privilege

TOKENS AND COINS

Tokens and coins, a game you can play
Not good and not evil, just spending your day
Cheaper than time, yet time they may buy
You flip 'em and try not to look where they lie

Coin with two sides is caught in a crack
You don't grab each side, then you won't get it back
Don't see both sides, then best go to school
Or find some religion, or go play some pool

More than one way, and still more than two
But start with a two-sided question for you
Why were you born and why are you here?
From now till you die what's your reason for fear?

Dollars or gold, or new BTC
It's only what's purchasing time that's for me
Time to sit down, to look in your eyes
And ask what the hell does it mean to be wise

THE MASSES

The masses enjoy a tempo
They like a rhythmic sound
Well-defined and regulated
Like the civilization now around them
So, here and there, we indulge their taste
Coat a gemstone in a trim little dress
It flows—sometimes the language of the gods
Sings in harmony with our own, a temple echo
But to you, not the masses—look in my eyes now
To you I say this
Between the tidy lines may be one
More rough, more subtle, more than a gemstone
A lump of molten energy
Mined from the belly of mother earth
Which declines to wear a pretty dress
Which burns their well-defined temples to ashes
Which presents itself akin to madness, mayhem
Thunderous storm in the palm of your hand
The potent masses may pass it over, but you
Take it in reverence, pass through it
Let its fearsome thunder pass into you

And you may one day feel

The fire of the gods

Blazing from your eyes

Lighting the way

To our next step higher

EYE OF DEATH

Eye of death, steady, I stand my ground
Chin up, hands ready to face you
My brothers don't know as I do, you are no man,
    sinister and grim
You are the sweet womanly fountain of us all

I hate how you take what I clutch in my fingers
Divine pieces I felt I shouldn't lose
Screaming pieces, ones attached to myself
You sweep them up a spiral stairway
We tremble in fear when we look in your eye
You tell us nothing we can fathom

I met you before once or twice, you drove me mad
You appeared as a dark-eyed temptress, irresistible
We maybe had a toss in the hay, your hair was red
And you were gone in the morning
Moved on to a man you really wanted
But in a dream, you came again, consummated,
    gave me these lines

Fearless, I see you now, your eyes are different

One becomes an impeccable green

The other a black hole, timeless, spaceless, free

And somehow, I realize, my hands loose

Without the clutching, without the hating,

I see in your eyes a sweet germination

A togetherness, a reconciled beginning

ODE TO THE OPERATOR

If pride may allow it
A nod to you, former comrade
Though I stood only a few short years beside you
I stand as an equal now to address you
Allow an open-eyed interlude to intrude
Between my noncombatant trances
Read a verse inexact, rocky, irregular
As your beard in Afghanistan
Men of ready force, side by side, men of few words
Men who mean just what they say
Your equal is hard to find outside our old halls
You, brave and dutiful surgeon of humanity
Slicing out the cancers we suppose must be excised
From the supposed body of supposed civilization
And what we suppose to be is often the case
And justified is your pride in the spear
Held by tradition in the massive hand of Odin
And yet I direct you to the eyeless socket
Where the old god traded his sight for wisdom
And by whose wisdom is the cancer now diagnosed?
By rulers unable to diagnose

their own collective insanity?

I implore you, old friend

Be attuned to your own diagnoses

As they are sung by the unmatched music

Of your sacred quiet soul

And reject them not if they one day say

"The rulers presume to understand a symptom

"And to prescribe an operation

"And thus bury ideas that built their pedestal

"Ideals that may heal an illness at last"

Step off on a day when you find that the halls

To and from your operating rooms

Have become upside down

For though a surgeon's skills and implements

Rightfully inspire a grateful awe

And guns give a deep exciting feel

An awfully deafening thunder

An unnatural rain of twisted destruction and steel

Heavy and urgent as these may be

How much higher the honor

When a surgeon one day

Having laid down his knife

Becomes a true healer

If pride may allow it

NEVER BE MINE

Never be mine, whoever you are
As I am never yours truly
When my nose itches, I will pick it
And when a law bores me, I will break it
And the moment you feel you own me
Is the moment my desire moves on to another
Though you may be nearer, dearer than life
Dear from a time that I saw you, wanted you
If I had wanted to own your spirit
I would not have been my truest self
And the animal that owned you
Would not be me truly
A soul is her own first possession
Her stranger properties are lower
Never including for one millionth of a second
Another soul
To your soul: I see you
My desire is toward your liberty
If liberty dies, so dies the passion
Meet me separately up here, break a law for me
Break it hard and rudely
And never be mine

EYELIDS SHUT

My eyelids shut, I see you reading me
And to you from these words I reach
My hand lies on your shoulder quietly
Warm forehead leaning on yours lightly
No care for the look or smell of your skin
Only your thoughts that are or may have been
I wish my hope into you, drawing near
Forgive me, permit me to breathe in your ear
"Live well, have joy, die well, my dear."

LOW-VOICED SIREN SONG

Clash and tumult, manly strife
Violent confrontation
"The highest way of life," one said
The rhythm of a war drum
I know their kind, and bear no grudge
I served a term among them

Smashing rhythm they present
A harmony magnetic
A pulse of life they hold within
A primal heart may get it
The young and restless turn to them
To feel the beat frenetic

They may sing their siren song
Centuries not dissuaded
And if you're shallow but you're strong
You'll find your spirit shaded
By trees through which you see no forest
Find your wisdom traded

Wisdom sold, willpower bought

A will made in their image

The rest of us resent you not

We may forgive the carnage

And one day when you're old and deaf

I hope you hear

     The dissonance in their melody

MEN WENT

Sing, "Men went to Catraeth at dawn"
As we have always gone
To inspire a song
And fatalistic phallic admiration

From Cambria to the Hindu Kush
A quickened pulse we push
Pierce and watch it gush
For why else build civilization?

And still the earth receives our blood
Not quite drunk in the flood
Bodies in the mud
A hero's silent destination

"The heroes and the cravens" both
The vultures never choke
Laugh the final joke
Unfazed by our disintegration

But if we lay some daffodils
From bloodied ancient hills
On our windowsills
Will children build a better nation?

HOW MUCH

How much of it is enough?

      How much will the deity want from me?

Will mine be too little? Too much?

How many drops of my sweat

      to distill our sacred melody?

And when I run dry, what will you get?

How much of the time in a year

      to lively run, or walk and breathe

How much may I watch and hear

a duel between action and breath?

      How much to be silent or speak?

Or revel in life, or wrestle with death?

How many trees do I plant you

      to shade our grandchildren's neighbors?

How much peace do I grant you?

Or how much challenge and growth?

      How much trading of favors

may bind us in truth and acceptance both?

How much remorse have I shirked?

    Saved away for a gray-haired day?

With how much joy could I work

if I cash out before the end?

    And if I take a payment today,

How much shall I withdraw, my friend?

BOOK 2

DIRT BROTHERS
AND OTHER POEMS

May – August 2021

INTRICATE INFINITY

An intricate infinity
A solid and a liquid free
Together form and fall apart
And form again, a beating heart

Insinuate, peek in and out
It's in the face and not too loud
A silence and a steady nerve
An essence of a spoken word

Don't try to know, just look and see
Don't try to do, but breathe and be
It runs away and comes again
And swirls around from now to then

Elaborate, it spouts a spring
A past and present reckoning
A future given, bold and wise
Infinity is in the eyes

A billion eyes all part of one

A brighter moon, a darker sun

Fragmenting here and fusing there

It pierces with a heavy stare

I know not what its name may be

It touches you and touches me

And from your eyes to mine it flows

And where it came from heaven knows

BLUE SPECKLES

Plodding with friends in a silent unholy night

Through pitch-black swamps in the piedmont

Senses taut, alert to play the game

Yet enamored with a dazzling other game at my feet

Each step in the muck awakens a tiny wonderland

Every fresh footprint dimly aglow

With the faint and subtle luminescence

Of miniscule blue speckles

Those vain night wargames now are near forgotten

But never will I forget, nor cease to smile

At the meek and mysterious memory

Of the glowing blue speckles at my toes

THEY THAT SOW IN TEARS

They that sow in tears may reap in carnal joys
May the harmless chickens come on home to roost
Let us gather up the eggs now, girls and boys
Let them sow a better seed in love and truth

They that grow a better garden soon may find
That a higher path is still a bed of thorns
And a tangle is not simply left behind
And a newer growth itself shall be reborn

They that made them sow in tears are dead and gone
Yet their good and evil still are in the land
And an enigmatic balance moves along
And the scales of justice yet conceal their hand

DAMP WARPATH

Red rain may wash and run
In vain too late to catch
A stain the color of a gun
Too wet to let you light the match

The sympathy has gone
It died a while back
No special wish to turn it on
Or light a fire of want and lack

Bedraggled to the bone
A soaking legionnaire
A stoic chin of cold enthroned
And steely lips which spit no care

In spittle of the drizzle
In pitch pines roam and ditch
An empathy too high and little
A silent violent fever pitch

In sleet and sludge you beat

A quiet single file

A trudging comradeship of feet

Drip callous deeds of malice vile

The other man deserves

The bloodshed in the rain

Cold platter of hot justice served

His mother must soak up the pain

An ice is in the vein

A vice you're bringing home

The nicer Romans might remain

But in your icy mind you roam

NIGHT ON THE STYX

Illusions of grandeur

Mirages in glitter

Night visions and fantasies

Flame and then wither

Rise and evaporate

Leaving a misty wake

Sleep on a hazy lake

Sink in a river

Currents that wind around

Hissing a heaving sound

Soaking a moving ground

Weaving forever

My grasping and glory

A wisp and a flitter

A flutter, a gasp of air

Burnt in a fever

A dancer all flowing

Full pouring out everything

Refusing to choose between

Water and fire

Hold her and leave her

Float to her undertow

Dying to live with her

Breathlessness give her now

Listen here

     I illuminate the dark below

     A hallucinating sparkle glow

     Intrude into a daydream daze

     Grip a vapor as it vaguely fades

Lights out on illusions

Clean out the shiny specks

Postponing a whirlpool

Refocus, what's next

Another evening will return

Strike out along her hazy banks

A watery fearsome blaze will burn

Remember pouring out your thanks

LIVING WATER

You wouldn't know that history ever happened
That people really did the things they say
You wouldn't need to hear or read about them
Until you spend some nights and days away
Adrift along the ancient waterways
Of old North Carolina

It may be something or it may be nothing
That wafts across your skin as sun goes down
That tingles down your spine as you encounter
An old black cottage way outside of town
A sense of generations come and gone
The crueler and the finer

A mountain sinking or a valley rising
An orphaned bird sings on a broken limb

A cruel accomplished fact won't rise for fighting

Or caring how they blame or judge the sin

Less-than-fine but flowing out to finer

A stream of living water

TO PLAY WITH DEATH

To play with death, breathtaking fling
A flirt, a spurt, a furious thing

While riding blind, you feel alive
Awake and daring to survive

She doesn't need a violent soul
To tease and please and rock and roll

A tingling tension, hard and free
A starkly colored world you'll see

Don't play too long; she'll break you in
And make you lose, and she will win

And when she wins, she'll bring you round
To lively seed her holy ground

I CAME, I SAW

"I came, I saw, I conquered"
But my conquering was vain
In vanquished eyes an empty prize
I lost to win the game
Survival of the civilized
Repress and hide the pain

The ancestors the conquerors
Descendants reap the gain
Resembling them, I walk their land
Laugh off the shallow blame
Hard ground of opportunity
A state of pride and shame

I came, I saw, release me
Come show me how to give
Confess the beast within me
To live and let you live

A better conquest bring me

Undo what fathers did

Your eyes no longer conquered

I came, I saw, I gave

I took only as offered

No owner and no slave

A blanket down, a softer ground

A land of free and brave

A freer conquest finding

To covet and to crave

A dusky lust unwinding

Unfold a rolling maze

Untie cathartic bindings

Unleash and ride the wave

TO A FALLEN BROTHER

Dust to dust

Thrust up an ashen smolder

Your embers flicker to the deep

Before today

The rain wept on your eyebrows

Green shoulders grown too rough to weep

From today

My showers damp your earth

My smoky growth recalls your shade

Your dusty road

At night I walk beside you

Flow through the opening you made

TORRENT

Bitter teardrops poured in a torrent

Of impossible pain rocked in your brain

Belly cramping down an empty vortex

No stemming the flow, no plugging the drain

You were the tree that fell in the forest

Let no one hear, the thunder is vain

Flooding up from a churning abyss

Salt stream of a bloody desperation

Low rumble rolled, scraped your soul

Lightning flashes a whip, self-flagellation

Seeking nothing attainable on this

Mere surface of oceans in motion

Little did you know

The hemorrhage broke a silent floodgate

Holding no longer down below

A thrust that no longer will wait

Done being strangled, beginning to sing

Empty abyss became a source

Filling with force, a freshwater spring

FRUIT'S PROCESS

A bright idea

Thrust a seed in mud

An urgent lust

Pierced an open bud

A purging rain

Drenched and drained the dust

A dirty work

Swelled an orb robust

Then to mature

Pure surrender cede

Capitulate

Wait to meet the need

DO YOU EVER HEAR IT?

Do you ever hear it?

Murmuring, vibrating, echoing

Through the ether, across the universe

Between waves of your existence

Might you remember it?

A straining hopeful tension

An old radio, Neil Young singing

A feeling of ache and renewing

Did you see it?

Pure flowing locks of fair hair

A child's curls are dimmer, flying off

Darkening into a vivid future

Can you feel it?

Whispering into your pores

Breathe out rhythmically from hair-ends

Tingling on the skin, percolating

Will you smell it?

Salty sweat, wet earth, summer steam

Bursting orgies of springtime growth

An aura of foggy life-force

Do you taste it?

Nations nurtured on the tip of a tongue

A bittersweet essence of old betrayal

Thick acidic flow of continuation

May we know its name?

I know nothing that may be stated

      As I hear the straining murmur,

      See and feel a flowing beat

      Smell and taste new spice and vapor

Owning a sensual momentum

Taking and tainting vitality herself

Be at peace for the hearing

Lustfully watchful to see

Grip and hold a tenuous sensing

Deeply breathe in selfish generosity

Seen from the lips, heard from the eyes

Read in a future language

Of colors flashing and flowing

Ever so silent and murmuring

Do you ever hear it?

FORGIVE ME

Forgive me please, my darker neighbor
For failing to use a season with you
Head bowed for the crimes of old fathers
Undoing unwelcome unfairness they sowed
Sorry won't sow oats, a land is ours today

Forgive me, soulful woman, black beauty
For never spending a full generation
Fully finding a fairer Eden
Melding our bodies together in shade
Into a healing pool of resolution

Let me sow the seed of an Eden
Form with me a river haven

Begin in my thickets, thorny vines weaving
Trudging and pulling a squeaky wagon
Excavate brown earth with me

Dig up a pond of bare cleansing

Well-stocked pool of swimming abundance

Let us attack an old tangle of unfair vines

Together we slash a path in the morass

Dash out from the weltering maze

To a field, red sorrel we may chew

A brighter field for me and you

To finally be free

A broader plain where I and the fathers

May finally be forgiven

IMMOVABLE PERSPECTIVE

Shall I rise with the sun to a daytime of doing?

Justify my existence by coming and going?

Shall I mind that activity passes for action?

Will mine be a privilege and thus become guilt?

Will our children be free in the homes we have built?

Shall I raise my hand continually

To feed any mouth that bites me?

The sun in the windowpane shining a smile

Upon my face, frozen in time for a while

Attempting here a motionless perception

Immovable perspective is the mission

Feel free to hate my economy of motion

But friend, if you believe I'll lie all day

We've never really met, have we?

Undeterred by your freedom, I continue my way

Stubbornly passing

Today's distractions

If I may be lazy, I'm lazy fully, actively

Without a frantic hurry, I seem to passively

Let a day pass while I focus internally

If you reject, reject me fatally for all I care

I make each move in a clearer air

And if my immovable perspective is wrong

I'll ride it into the ground before long

FROM THE GROUND

The voice of your brother's blood
Cries out to me from the ground
A rut, a pit that you dug
A tongue in silence is bound

Your light extinguished tonight
Another is shining below
You think you're awake; are you right?
Till you die, you never will know

A kindred future cut out
A similar soul you rejected
They tell you that you should be proud
His light is there lying neglected

You'll follow your brother in time
He sees and knows you outside it
Your pit feeling real in your mind
Too real tonight to abide it

But I am your brother who's dead

The blood is drained and dry

His resting peace is in my head

Wake up and look in my eye

I've come to you from the ground

My tongue drips onto this page

You did what you did, I went down

I've forgotten resentment and rage

Come down with me tonight

My killer, come die with me

Switch on my humbler light

Tomorrow you'll start to see

YEZIDI WEDDING

Till my dying day I recall them

When I ever see a clanging flash

A laughing color

A sparkling stream of merriment

In a dusty land of fear

Defiance of the hate surrounding

Jubilant new love, its vigor surviving

Caravan of vehicles to the horizon

Horns all honking, relatives and friends

Neighbors dancing in pickup beds

Each girl and woman decked out, exquisite, beaming

Hoots and hollers, gunshots in the air

Exuberant surge of gathering, mixing

Rebuke to a stern reality around them

One truck after another

Through spring in southern Kurdistan

Up the road from Tal Afar, up a sacred mountain

Kurmanji greetings thrown to strangers and to foes

Smiling waves for me, nameless foreign soldier

Sweets and love spread round like pollen

Oblivious to animals prowling the border

Ignorant of devastation soon to come

Impervious now to life's brevity and harshness

A shimmering burst of humanity's hearty joys

A wedding among the Yezidis

THY NEIGHBOR'S WIFE

"Thou shalt not covet," was commanded
And good and golden is the phrase
Until it pushes heavy-handed
Don't crave your neighbor's wife, it says

So many questions swirl about me
My neighbor may be a generous man
Whose wife's ennui may swell without me
To crave her as only a stranger can

And what if she decides tomorrow
To have her cake and eat it too?
She'll not be stolen, maybe borrowed
For just one night, or maybe two

Commandment noted, rise above it
No ox or donkeys graze on this road
My neighbor has no servant to covet
Millennia have lightened the load

Now here she comes in that jogging outfit

Teasing because she knows he sees

For all his ego, beneath and around it

A coveted wife is the wife he needs

And so I work in the yard half naked

And play the part of a macho man

My eye on her body says, "Let me take it

And thrill you more than the old man can"

I covet not the owning of her

But only imagine a casual date

And hope he doesn't own her either

Nor mind too badly her coming home late

DIRTY MIND

A dirty mind, deplorable rhymes
A libertine ahead of my times
Perhaps I missed a hippie moment
When future was new and unruly and fine

I'll clean it up when duty demands
And wear the hat and march in the band
If playing the game may bring us together
And show my intention in pure open hands

The gesture only is all I can do
Then skip to the forest away from you
I'll take off the mask and bask in the mud
It runs in my blood and I'll carry it through

MELTING

Will a melting pot finally melt?

Will a charge of harmony harshly be felt?

Sharp smoke of a pipe, passing around

Laughing together, sit on the ground

Will you finally mean

The peace that you say?

Night into day, fear melting away

Raging voice inside

Falling shriveled and tiny

Give way to a booming unity mighty

My pot is so little, outside I don't know

Which way the world may finally go

But here in my trees, I smell and I see

The melting of you and the melting of me

REFLECTING POND

Reflecting pond, too still for comfort

Mosquitos love you and men avoid you

Until I spied your image today

You quietly mimic meandering clouds

Mirror the top of a longleaf pine

The muddy flop of a frog

Little murky ripples, sparkling specks

I resist the wish to lean and see myself

The truth already is mine

My life is larger than yours

Yet you challenged my comfort under the pines

You offered a fresh and fluid feel

A damp and dimming, reassuring weight

A gleaming and still reflection

DIRT BROTHERS

Come share the land with me

Stomp a warpath under her trees

She's a mystical land

Each acre welcoming me and you

We brethren who gratefully tread them

The dirt in our hands, brother

The land is a deep mother

Let's savor her progeny

Lay our fatigue in her shade

Let her be our goddess

We'll worship together

And wait for the fool coming

Daring to threaten her

Blindly abusing her

We'll crush him in fury

Make of him a sacrifice to fertilize

The dirt that made us brothers

READ ME THRICE

Read me thrice, and I'll go with you
First in a daybreak clear and bright
Aloud amid songbirds' careless romping
Alone or connected, tranquil with coffee
Read me in open tones of the morning

Pore again my lines in a pavilion
Surrounded by downpour turbulence
Barely sheltered, dimly lit porch or gazebo
Tiny whirlwind droplets assault my pages, glowering
Read me and weep the sweet juices of flowing release

A third time, read me in the still night, not crying
But soaked in the afterglow of your passions
Foreshadow the sweet release of dying
Read me distinct to yourself or your lover
Or to me, a dead man attentive
I won't mind as we walk along
An anxious city street or moonlit crickets' lane

Three times read me

Three perfect moments spend with me

And somewhere out here

Perhaps I will smile

And delight to see you smile with me

MR. STRANGER'S HARVEST

Rough and ready

Tough and steady

Stranger wears a sunburnt hide

Food he grew her

Never knew her

Saw her by a husband's side

Till she spied him

Dignified him

Smothered by an owner's pride

Spark inside her

Dark desire

Dreams on fire in her mind

Hard and heavy

Raw and sweaty

Came the stranger to the bride

Pleasure shaking

Harvest taking

Karma will not be denied

Mr. Stranger

Free of danger

Someone else's turn to hide

People frowning

Feelings drowning

Sweeping outward in the tide

Neighbors meeting

Smiling greeting

Secrets keeping deep inside

BANDAGE

When a runaway focus becomes an obsession

Helpful habit becomes an obstructive addiction

A shot in the arm

A bid to escape

A rush and a thrill

Take on a new shape

Soothing bandage is dripping in medicine's tingle

Seeping open while blood and eternity mingle

But peel off the wrap

The wound is now closing

You're needed up top

The dawn is approaching

RESENTING AND SATISFACTION

Try not to resent them

The loud tone deafness of calloused neighbors

They cannot help failing to absorb

The beauty that passes them by

As I can no longer help being attuned

To something of bizarrely startling colors

Where coherence won't sufficiently enter

A brightness prose can no longer address

Against my will tuned in at noon

Do not resent my writing out the contrast

For myself and those who may hear its tune

I say what I can before dying satisfied

Try not to resent the routine drag

For being dull and gray

But close your eyes to see a thrilling sight

A ripe persimmon distinct in a naked tree

A clear delineation, one against an opposite

Juxtapose before and after blending

Starker strokes to milder shades

Bolder forces clash in daylight hotness

Fade into an evening tug-of-war

Unnatural-seeming contest, never evil

Imagine these behind a daily dullness

Your clash becoming real beyond the drag

And one day it may be more sharply so

Resent not the state of the union around you

Frustrated strangers pass on the street

Public frustration, heavy-handed state

The future comes and goes again

And history took and gave and went

Things done no longer touching you

Sherman's march was here for them

But now is neither here nor there

On Sherman Drive you find a fine house

Play ball with children in the yard

While angry strangers pass you by

Resent only what bars your own mind

From working magic with invisible hands

Even you, frustrated brother

Wishing to listen while tone-deaf

Ah my groans, hearing them one day sooner

May have barred you from murder

Yet if you at last tune in and hear me

Then end the resenting then and there

And pour me out a toast on the ground

And give a private laugh of satisfaction

FALL OF 1898

The nadir of the story of a state
Worst days our longleaf pineland ever saw
October and November of 1898
A knot that held for decades not untying
A bruise that maybe always will be raw

My fathers then in poverty in Wales
Oblivious to Fayetteville's unease
But here now on this soil, I'm feeling out the tale
        The brothers of the sandhills set to rising
But then were beaten back onto their knees

Don't make me look away from wrecking trains
Perhaps the Reconstruction had its ills
But what they did in Wilmington, how can you
explain?
A century or two, cut bandage still unwinding
Perhaps by 2098 we'll heal

The sun beats down, an old town road ahead

The darkest shade may rest in peace behind

No sundown towns, the Red Shirts now are dead

A sweeter bruising future is delicious

A basket bound together, ever kind

MACHINE

He grew up almost naturally
Reaction to traffic, kudzu by a highway
Sprouted like a weed from concrete activity
In human weakness he found his way

Useful gears and pistons proliferate
Metal lines assemble a mindless state
For us fitting into him, useful we feel
Pressed into service, a hamster wheel
Feeding a beast that will eat our children
Even the outcast ones on the margin
We fuel a rat race to devil-knows-where
And we'll all be dead before he gets there
Worn out and spent to our bones
Under his wheel we are cobblestones
His concrete poured over fields and woods
Unless we disengage for good
Will we finally find his natural limit?
If a light is too bright, you know you can dim it

Even the most relentless wave

Waxes only so far and then wanes

And is it too much for me to pray

The machine and his concrete may do the same?

DAWN IN THE BADLANDS

My comrade still asleep

In the canyon of a creek

When climbing up and out, my life begins

The sun that calls my name, a newfound friend

Dazzling cold droplets on prairie grass

Frost on a buffalo patty I pass

Early bison over there on the hill

Munching his rhythm, enjoying the chill

Rubbing my eyes and stretching, I stand

Cluster of sagebrush delighting my hand

Nostrils flaring, clearing my ears

A mountain sheep's horn I find lying here

My steps, questioning, tracing the brink

Of a canyon cliff, simply to listen, I think

Or look, or smell the air of a wilderness

Searching and soaking in morning awareness

Relive the bold rainbow an evening before

Awakened in all my five senses and more

The horizon is mine in every direction

A canyon that winds, water's chilly reflection

Each part of my body, the thrust of my mind

Piercing this moment, making it mine

Drinking eternity even through time

For that is the strength of the plains at dawn

May my sunrise walk go incessantly on

May the wolves of last night stay barely at bay

As we saunter the hills this glorious day

RAMPAGE

Storming across the Sahara

Grizzled men with twisted manes

Rampaging along with messier friends

Dark denizens of barren plains

Loaded land cruisers bristle with guns

Ripping out at a reckless pace

Grinning and laughing in eager freedom

Dust flying high in our jagged wakes

Waving to wild and wandering camels

Camp at night on a rugged course

Uneasy company of flies and scorpions

We pass a wreck and bones of a corpse

Forgotten fighter, one of our kind

A blip in a measureless wilderness

Bleaching beside the tanks and landmines

Grim rebuke in a desert of nothingness

Scale a sharp rock in the vacant air

Scrape the flint and spark the steel

Roast a goat and eat up there

Survey the wasteland's infinite field

Sheer and defiant, uncaring and hard

It bears us along, we wander for days

Seeking the mountains we saw from afar

Rampage in the desert and learn of his ways

THE RACES

A starting gun fires, the races are on
Fire up the party, turn up the song
Why should I walk? Time for running along

Run down the good life, run up the next hill
Run on through the ages, imposing your will
The strongest of runners inspire the crowd
Inventors of empires, sprinters are loud
The loss of a hero, a sacrifice grave
Then rushing to fill the hole that he made
All moving as one, and keeping straight on
On to the melee, on to the next song
Away from the animal deep in your bones
And on past humanity's musing and tomes
A race, who can be the best robot today?
A wager that nature survives while we play
The starting gun's bullet is falling back down
It slams only inches away in the ground

Next to a dandelion, in among remnants

Of signs and banners and emblems and pennants

A sign saying "Racetrack" is crumbling away

"It all was a sprint," hear the dandelion say

The marathon run by a fountain of life

Sweeping our dust and our rushing and strife

Why should I walk? Why shouldn't I hear

The dandelions over the guns in my ear

More bullets are slamming, too far and too near

MY TREES

Surreal yet crisp, in a dream I saw clearly
As a marveling boy it came to my spirit
Deep in a swamp under ponderous trees
Stump of an oak once admired by druids
Old shade of a medicine man's uncertainty
A hatchet stuck in it, stump so wide and comforting
Life is still in it, but not its good old life
Thorny vine crops out the top, rebellious, insolent
It pokes me; I snip and pull, yet it sharply returns
Feeling for the sky, searching for shadowy infinity
Pricking and painfully mocking your dull society

Though dying, the stump refused to be tame
In my heart, though a boy, I felt the same
My love for the stump lit up like a flame

And the dark mystery of the thorny vine
Intrigued me to know it would never be mine
But jut out into darkness for all of time

Then waking to a neighborhood of dullness

Forgotten stumps under ugly houses

I determined to one night return to my trees

Can you not glean from a dream

An uncertain climbing vine?

If not a million acres wild, free and open

At least give me a few stumps

Of ponderous and swampy mystery

HUM

What is the hum in your ears

That comes and goes at times in the night?

Once intensely ringing

Again a vague pulsating buzz

Pressing near, so deep inside yet far away

Question it, my friend

Does it scan creation's waves?

Or ripple plainer, symptom of old explosions

Perhaps a tenuous balance, tip of a needle

Between staring down a shattering blast

And wailing dismay at cruel futility

Here tonight vibrate in your skull

Dull pains of your past

Scraping and scratching to the here and now

Glide into harbor in your ancient brain

Might it warn of immediate tension

Dull dehydration, heat of today

Or a memory of something before birth

Be neither glad nor disturbed when it comes in

Nor unhappy nor relieved when it fades

It will visit you again

Humming softly to your mind

In its horrible beauty and strain

Listen curious and distantly

Feel it, whatever it is

Before it falls away silent

THE SHATTERED

It's still broken, mama, glue won't bind

Who can help? I can't remake it

The perfect way it used to shine

How on earth did we let them break it?

Why couldn't we all just leave it alone?

It seemed to be like ice when it shattered

Can't remember how it looked, but I loved it

So bright and calm, nothing else mattered

A language, a tribe, nothing was like it

Why didn't we make each other stop?

Why didn't we turn and listen, mama?

Why all the fighting to be on top?

It's all in pieces

We pushed to acquire

And use it roughly

Until it expired

I keep on trying

Now it's too cold

Hot glue is drying

It doesn't hold

Mama, are you there?

Maybe cold silence

And a vacant stare

Gave birth to a violence

What on earth

Can anyone do

To put it together

Or make it new?

PUSHING TONGUE

Floated in slowly, then sowed and settled
A hopeful weed, or a hive of bees
Bustling barbs, a stinging nettle
Pushed in on the water, from the east

A tangle outgrown, a strident sound
Ejecting old echoes, asserting itself
Sharp growth that flowed across the ground
Fated to take a forest's wealth

Tall and spreading a shadow rough
Six centuries ago now
Pushing the natives west and north
Overshaded the neighbors somehow

Strangled the bards, then wooed the highlands
Five centuries in a romantic past
Stuck the north and ruled the island
How rough the wooing became at last

Triumphal tongue all tall and proud

Pressing a kingdom into a hive

Push now west, test new ground out

The Tuscarora may not survive

Overrun three centuries ago

Forest tongues of fading pain

Funny what simple descendants know

Forgotten sound echoing in the brain

Old languages lost or hang by a thread

A buckskin Scot in an Indian gang

Defying the hive and waking the dead

A silence is broken, a swamp regained

But louder this hopeful tongue of union

It sailed the globe and drowned the rest

Pushing, absorbing each syllable human

Save those which into a silence it pressed

And now by its sting you read my mind

Or a syllable ancient I found in a dream

Weep not for the echoes we left behind

Sharp sounds come around

Yet flow as a stream

TIME LOOPING

What did we see tomorrow?

And what are we planning now for yesterday?

Will we go new places a year ago?

Did the rain fall up to the clouds

When your tenth descendent was born?

I take and I touch and I grip

And so say that I know what it is

Till the day that it flows or it drips

Through fingers near and unfamiliar

Neither mine, nor hers, nor his

How will they frame the query

The quest to grasp a flow

A goal to clasp reality's collar

To feel we somehow know

Which way we went tomorrow

SCREECH

How screechingly I may have flailed

Wreak havoc in a gale about my face

Unhesitating ripping ream the shreds

Allotted single voice all portioned out

Until indelible abatement snatch an eye

Split-second pause and whirl aflame aloft

The stocky legs, a stomp and blurry crash

A pounding fist of bark all flaking out

My ragged sandy parchment paper throat

A stream of screaming evils flung on high

A smacking smoke of chaos surging long

Harsh raging harking hailing not a word

I peel the ranging toxin out the pores

Jaw yawning force a bullhorn cracking up

Shout off the fated clouds and dare the sun

Come dry up all the terrors I have wrought

Howl down a hard renouncing now in all

A screeching stop

Relinquishing tornados of the soul

But that's enough of me.

How was your day?

BLANK

Just it

That one

Nothing there

But smooth everything

A creamy hue denying gaze

Continued haze

See not

On along

Exhale

Fade out

NEXT

What's next today now
Strain to find
Through stormy rubbish
Of the lines
A cackling maniac
In my mind

I owe them something
Unsure how
To find a duty
Here and now
Uncover rulers
Learn to bow

Beneath the nonsense
Grope alone
Conveyor open
In my home
A lean to leap out
Freely roam

ORIGIN

Unstructured flow

Unplanted flag

A rooted firmament unfurled, a speck

Stick on a pinprick poise

Though thick is a thumbprint finger pad

Thorny berry centered on a spot

To shooting up a junkie into space

A float of firmer words

Evading every memory

Sayings earlier than tongue conceived

Protein flows heavy and lightly free

Downstream as a leaf

Time flirted with space

Now stuck in the dirt

A slurring vision burrowed

Launchpad invisible visiting earth

Dripping, unfolding in a stroll

Unroll and scribble a scroll

Before a parchment was

Unfold and hold a gliding marble eternity

Deep purple, a gurgling bubble of death

A blackness of origin

Back to write on white again

EROSION CONTROL

Block it in, plant some grass
Silty soil will wash out fast
Can't allow the trending down
To undermine the whole damn town

Fence it in, protect the work
Lazy bums will try to shirk
Erode our values and our gains
Wear away our growing pains

Keep it separate, neat divide
Stay in your lane on your side
Don't erode our straighter lines
With squiggly scribble undermines

Shore it up, define the words
Our language going to the dogs
Culture changing, slow it down
Too much laughing, someone frown

Regulate it, push it out

Control a substance if too loud

Can't allow a sloppy rhythm

To undermine the whole damn system

Separate tables, stop the mix

The neighbors mingling, got to fix

Define the terms, divide us up

Each with his own bowl, spoon and cup

The sand is flowing through the hole

You idiot so in control

The system served a structured style

Your high-and-tight, your shallow smile

The ground has dropped; it's high enough

Embracing the forbidden stuff

And laughing off the walls and rules

To rule the soil, a game of fools

UNDULATING LIFE

What is a lower life

If not a drop in an ocean undying?

Falling from where

Flowing to where

We know without knowing

We fire up a boiler

How to steam higher

A dogged plodding of science trying

And lazy assuming religion vying

A vexing tangle presuming, lying

What is a higher life

If not one seeking to see the ocean?

Cresting a wave

Searching the grave

We hear without seeing

Dim vision arriving

The steam higher rising

In dying I find a cathedral ceiling

All squirming and squealing and one day revealing

A rush of not knowing now slowing and healing

What is a reaching life

If not a cell in an ocean's mind?

By ending begin

Evaporating

A cloud lightly passing

To simulate early

Smoke viciously swirling

A poison enlightens while making you fade

Both darkens and brightens while steaming away

A life in a mirror, a wave of the day

TOMORROW AT DROWNING CREEK

Only on the verge of a probability of death

If jokes and bravado sink silent for a moment

Does the word "love" rise and float

You hear a comrade with new ears

And smell in him a swimming piece of you

Soon to be cut off from shallow laughs

And from the body where your ears reside

Cling to a linking root upon the bank

Of a river Jordan you will cross unaided

A lonely drowning creek for all you know

On the verge you say or think the rafts you mean

In him see every piece you leave behind

And hear a harmony you should have made

With all the floating pieces up till now

And if the verge of the bank should fade away

And death decline to materialize today

Words of linking and their buoyancy may go

Returning to the pebbles of before

You skip the stones and go on your way

And recognize again only the shell in the mirror

Of one silent piece residing in your skin

But it doesn't need to be that way tomorrow

Meet me at the Jordan again, maybe we'll see

That brunette killer dance in her red bikini

And we'll jump in eagerly this time

A floating laugh

And try to die together

NOD TO DYLAN

Neither time nor tide may wait to heal a wound

Sweeter smell of rain fells age's pale fence

You may measure tides in minutes and in moons

Where in salty muck a rail of recompense

Oozing boon from hell of doldrums, good in doom

Head is shaking in an ear-itch, hide the fight

Gray decaying clay of fate too late to judge

Even mama's lazy boy might save the night

Day communing with a worm of slime and sludge

Squeezing syllables to serve an eerie light

Staying not, bewilder raising glass dismay

Raging quiet on a diet baffled shine

Wait to punch a vivid point or paint your way

With a clicking rhythm scuttle drip the spine

Higher tides than mine too quick did flick away

HEARTY HANDSHAKE FOR WALT

Our hairy knuckles drag together
Across the Rockies, blast away dainty grains of dust
Cresting the peaks, we taste of tomorrow's daydream
Your reckless generosity my feast
Windy chuckle at a gruff joke held aside
Your full-bore booming echoed
In the valley down the years
Sweat and sloth and all embracing
Never lost on my spirit in the sun
You faced the blood, waded deeper than needed
Saying it broad and loud as a bearded rooster
Hit heavy a bit on the sunburnt nose
Spread all upon the menu of the land
The body and the grit in every strand
With knuckles bloody red and white
Blue collar scuffed and worn
You built the sturdy table
And spread it with the colors of us all
I lean my elbows on it with a burp
Others lay the dishes hard on your handiwork
Now I dare to bring today's meat

NAMING OF A CHILD

From now on down the halls of history
A prim pronunciation
A tongue in cheek and lips all twisting
Define your designation

Two syllables or five or twenty
Condense into your label
A wish for strength or smarts or plenty
Appointed from the cradle

Don't let it fool your future visions
Of who you are becoming
Your beating heart and spark of heaven
Eternal still is running

You came to us from God-knows-where
Some life is in the letter
We name a title you may wear
Yet never as a fetter

And when you're older you may honor

Or even rise above it

But underneath, if looking longer

You'll see yourself, and love it

ON PINS AND NEEDLES

On pins and needles, a boy sitting still

Endure the long words of wooden church pews

Impeccably mispronounced with certainty

Beneath a white steeple towering over piney woods

Loud preacher above pronouncing

Not a wandering doubt in his mind

That the wine in the Book was not real wine

That computer screens were a lazy hazard

And beware a lady's treacherous legs in short skirts

Until the longed-for shortened words arrive

"Atonement" and "Prayer" and "Amen"

To run into the sun and piney woods

At one in a prayerful moment amending

Mispronunciations into a fluent forest shade

Glancing back at the empty steeple shell

Through pines full of living sap

Quiet for walking on humble needles

With a tiny crackle whispered ever so prayerfully

Where the preacher shot his animals for sport

Not hearing the needles chuckle at the little steeple

As a walking boy shook his head

At the noise and whitewashed certainties behind

And wondered where to go on piney needles

MOLE SCRATCHING

There's a mole scratching his way

In my foundation tonight

Where he's going and why, he wouldn't tell

Doubtless he knows

But I'll have to murder him tomorrow

Blue glow in the vein drowns out what I meant to say

A homeless man was yelling out nonsense

Tuft of hair crops out

Mocks the way I was trying to behave

Wall firm-founded yet moving, attempting in vain

Presented mistakenly, power mortar chipped away

Outside of control, in the cool dark air

Is a chance for happiness, but only a chance

A mole scratching his way in my happiness tonight

Happy foundation is a mocking laugh

Night-covered man fancies himself a poet

Where he's going and why, he wouldn't tell

His skin-covered shadow may murder him tomorrow

DUEL

The devil from the deep
The angel in the skies
The wool of spotless of sheep
Is pulled across the eyes

A cloud of pearly white
To dazzle and to fool
Set day against the night
Dividing thus, to rule

The flesh against the heavens
The mind against the matter
The flatbread hates the leaven
The slimmer hates the fatter

The sheep may hate the devil
And see him everywhere
But where they choose to level
Their hate, he's rarely there

A tongue all forked and splitting

Divided angels laughed

The game forever pitting

The right against the left

Both hands of cloudy downpour

The pearly to the deep

Wet devils work together

To sow and then to reap

Dark soaking wool is harsh relief

A shroud drops showers to bequeath

A vision unified beneath

SOAKED IN COHERENCE

Stick your finger stopping leaky squirts

Of inconsistency

Conjure up adult coherent verse

Log cabins in the sea

Perceiving not the limits of the logic

That darks a damming wall

Consistent as a mortar for to clog it

Or block a waterfall

Pretend there is no end, a sleepy tonic

A ceiling on us all

If the ego surge in free relief

Across a boyish page

Do you judge me then a bloody thief

Or understand the rage?

When the ego fades to nothingness

Suspending disbelief

Will you box it as androgynous

To cap a light beneath?

They may mock it as unmanliness

And dam and plug the leak

If I build a wall of blind and deaf

As all the others do

Lock up the ego and his death

And play a game for you

Waves wouldn't crash or sound retreat

I'm blue in holding breath

No icy freeze or blazing heat

No origin is left

No Eden fruit, no grazing meat

Humanity bereft

The dams not slammed by mannish waves

Or breached too rude and broke

Refuse the use of youthful raves

A boy who bears no yoke

But leather cuts and tattoo hides of sailors

Reducing life to smoke

Rebuffing, lift no weight of wave impalers

But prod and push and poke

The dangling demi-man Olympus scalers

Poseidon's sirens woke

If you're baked enough

Get out of the oven

The demigods have only but

Half-kitchens on the mountain

With jumping-off rocks

For churning in a female ocean

Log cabins are their toys

The brawling thunder boys

Your broken finger is their booming joke

FREE-FLOATING FRAGMENTS

Free-floating fragments of myself

I watch you weave and drift

Winding along sidewalks

Lightly float to lie on the forest floor

Each along a new trajectory

To and from an old abode

Back to the all-holding hole

Where we used to swim together

The sounds you make now

On your way down

Are not yet my own familiar sounds

I love you from a distance

So float down your free-flowing color

And deny me not my distant path

I like to float far and see

The swimming hole from a separate angle

TO FEEL

To feel a steely cage of balance rounding

To a flux of flurried race

Where madness holds a knowledge circling sense

And one will win or else the other

The pull into a molten core

Or the spin out in a black abyss

And winning will but lose the next time round

As gravity will find another magnet

Where the puzzle pieces shuffle to each other

To suck away the knowledge out of time

Or matter chart a smarter course tomorrow

Though stumbling on a stump along the path

And a brush will paint itself around in circles

With a gush of horrid loss you felt down here

Though down and up and loss are but illusions

And to win is but a children's story game

Only in excruciating lonely fusing

Steel cages are dismantled one by one

Till the flurry be a slurry quiet dying

And the last cage snowy melt

To senseless spin away

And straighten out the feeling

ACHING BULLET

The deepest aching word won't touch the heart of it
A bullet in a brain was but the start of it
My throbbing splinter shovel dug too far to quit
But where's my bullet, raging quiet?

The dollars and the pennies making slavery
A mortgage and a fence became the fate of me
No dirty girls, tight penalty for family
But where to crow when hens out-crowd me?

If clawing in with aching skin I tie my noose
A clammy grave down in the roots of being loose
I cock the hammer, lock the banter, what's the use
But where to lay my walking boots?

A coward soul may never know how dark the night
In woods the crickets riot and a cock will fight
A spirit never right won't play your game so tight
But where to quiet the playing riot?

Kindly shoot me through the chest a shotgun blast

If you want then tell my sons their father passed

A life of sober goodness or your moral test

But where's my dirty girl, I ask

I used to have them, they dug into me and rode

My future tall and short, the blood and throbbing
showed

Another future's here, a long and stifling road

Where did my soul unload and go?

Onto a page of aching words you think are me

A silent surface of surprise attacks you'll see

The blaze of glory waits for later screaming free

I save a bullet for myself

The dullest aching game I stay around and play

Far down the road the day they shoot my soul away

Back to the riot games of loose and raging ways

As quiet in the dirt I lay

COLOR CANCELING

Pick your poison, take a side, the loony sayings go

Red juice or blue? There is no purple anymore

Forget the older colors, go lock the medicine cabinet

No neurosurgeon drugs, it isn't rocket science

Just take the bitter pill and join the fight

Yet I swear to God I saw a good evening

In an angry Pennsylvania cloudburst edge

The sky a full and urgent purple

Ill universal pimple of eons welling

Yearn to spurt in lunacy multicolored

Nothing of nature rejecting

Nothing to do with fleshy rocket surgery

Which they say is great nowadays

Universe full of our ancient ills brings a neighbor

Who wants to cut his off and have us pay

They demand I say the befuddled word

Or "her" armies hoist a pixelated flag

To say the word or not? Are you for it or opposed?

Beehive mind of pixel data in a two-toned cloud

And someone's daughter hates a macho world

But by God, you'd better call her "sir"

Or all of your goodwill the cloud declares is null

The pimple is there; will you pop it?

Arrayed on an overcast plain of battle

Old militia of pale ancient illness

Against the eager champions of a symptom

As I sit with my morbid rocket in between

Filled with goodwill on the grass, I pick a blade

It turns between the lines translucent violet

I refuse all poison pills in pouring rain

To chew the dripping strip of grass

As cellphone zombies trample me to puddy

And I mumble, smiling sunny

"Look, there's still purple. Isn't that something?"

LOOK OUT THERE — HOLD ON

Look out there — hold on

Let the one that has no glass window

Step out, throw the first stone

Glass holding on, half full in twilight

Lower than dawn overflow that filled it

Killed it, two birds, one stone on the sill

Plexiglas saved, upgraded the day, slick

Two fateful windows of a soul

What the hell will the tosser tell so late?

Fluently mute when some nights fall

Lower level, hurling devil, heavy as midnight

Lobbing darts at a far stone wall

This dark pitch won't pass the frontal lobe

Inhale; let it sink as a stone

Heave first the sundown round the globe

Then blow closer to lowly home

Nothing near can be stated now or later

Barely here a thing tossed on a paper

Holding alone a language all shattered

Slumping dumb on a floor of gray clay

Thrown on a stone threshold, reading glasses

Let a duct tape translator go home late

No sharper shard in rays of dusk

No smarter word that passes

Than a hefty breath and a step out a window

Throwing away the jagged weights

Into a night wind blowing

IT IS HARD

It is hard for you to kick against the pricks

In rusting junkyards walled around in crumbling bricks

Sticks and stones won't break your bones, but words may hover

A green-eyed turtle, bear the burden of your cover

A nameless pain, a biting bane, no one can tap it

Gnawing mouse inside your house up in the attic

It is hard for you to scream against your nature

Deny a dream, defy a dread, and meet your maker

She will distill this in the stillness, gentle rain

And linger ringing, singing rust into your brain

Deaf drag along a laughing song to keep from weeping

Blind crust around a hardened ground of grief in keeping

It is hard for you to stand on legs of jelly

Or hobble faster when the master is your belly

Stony words may prick and hurt, raw onion morsels

A crude divorcing dumb conventions of the turtles

They wobble on, their blinders on, and pull the carriage

Rusting skids under a broken pallet marriage

It is hard for you to bear the weight and move

It is hard forever chasing what to prove

It is hard to never know which way to kick

It is hard, the heat is heavy, air is thick

So let it hover just one day behind your eyeballs

Oil shining through the brine and rust of nightfall

Words and thoughts and into silence and to feeling

Let the layers of the onion get to peeling

LAUGH AT THE LETTERS

Pour a footer, let it cure

Set a post upright

Plumb it up and bolt secure

Level, sound and tight

In a season all your structure well-begotten

Will be vacant and outdated and forgotten

Take a moment to laugh at the level

Form a venture, take a risk

Build the world anew

Making that to rival this

Reaping what is due

In a season all the sweating growth and making

Will be obsolete and worthless and forsaken

Take a moment to laugh at the papers

Wear new clothing, wash the car

Take some pride in looks

Presentation gets you far

Sleek from head to foot

In a season the respect and admiration

Will forget you ever lived or looked amazing

Take a moment to laugh in the mirror

Write a poem, craft a verse

Weave an artful strain

Muse's song repeat, rehearse

Print and show your name

In a season all the seeds that you are planting

Are replaced or shaded by a higher ranting

Take a moment to laugh at the letters

BALLAD OF GEORGE MOSES HORTON

Well, I used to get a feeling
And let the feeling go
Not so with a wiser neighbor
He walked and let it flow
I heard about Mr. Horton
Pen made his paper glow
Out of pain he made a name
In a domain we ought to know

Domain of a shadow
Of chains and Chapel Hill
Longleaf pine above a battle
Walk a minefield of the will
He used to think about freedom
Used to muse how it ought to be
I wish old George were here
And maybe walk all day with me

Stroll out your soul

Poet George, poet George

Step out your harmony

A dream of something more

People thought he was low class

Those people all are fools

You know poet George was the finest hiker

To meet the longleaf muse

TO AN APPALACHIAN MEDICINE
WOMAN

are these my selfish

hotwire live hormones

given by mother earth

too gruff and grizzly

to hook your taste

you and i yet share

a dearth of privacy

but the city bots

will never stem

your leaner flow

keener dip and draw

deep-drinking mother of

a mountain soul

my only birthright

long and ringing beat

of a bearded

fire-stoking strand

my facial skin

may match dead men

whose paling depredations

you deplore

i am not you

and am not them

and we are each

a portion of the other

this portion saw

and heard

and found in you

sharing together more

than you may wish to grant

yet understanding

if my foreign warpath

leaves me on a shelf

here's bowing to you

a mother greener than

a bell-ringing son

myself

NAMELESS

When that which was nameless
Is given a name
Utility gained is more than equaled
By something different lost
Unspeakable properties

When that which was furious
Is tethered and tamed
To cultivate, save, or earn a living
A fuller field is burnt away
Invisible livelihoods

Our habitat harshness
Inevitable
I name and I tame a feral field
Defy my species for a night
Remember the nameless past

A nameless returning

Will come back around

Go toppling down the tethered titles

And if my memory serves me right

The game will begin again

HOMO SAPIENS IN BIT AND BRIDLE

Homo sapiens in bit and bridle

Plod along the rut

Glitter blinders and the reins won't idle

Proud and shafting trot

A convention rented from the scrolls

Dusty pages of the ages

Ring around the downy pillow rolls

Feather mattresses of cages

In a filly dream I met your bride

In a nightmare you met mine

In saddle wake resume our pride

Metal fence to ride the line

In the mind you gallop lighted plains

Or swing to juice the trees

Narrow mare of speed our prism gains

Fleshy key between the knees

Only hoping in our bridle pains

A beaming dream to squeeze

BACKWARD

How do you flip backward

In a calendar?

A thread unraveled

Won't spool again and fit the same.

How do you address

An old deity no longer believed in?

No making sense of what's gone.

Which words will be heard?

Where is the salvation

Of a language no one nearby will use?

Where is the recipe

Of a dish not eaten in centuries?

Where is the returning?

Will you find it in the blood?

Some may be in there

Where you'll never get it back.

The root is where it was

Since before a year was measured.

The land never belonged to blood.

She never owned the blood,

Yet you may belong to her again,

And when you do, you'll know

How she gives every thread and spool

At the moment when you need it,

Although her rough bark may bite,

Her weather drive you back to the present,

No need for flipping backward

In a calendar.

TO GRAMPA

Nid wyf yn gwybod Cymraeg

Peidiwch â gofyn imi ynganu hyn

Rwy'n gwybod ei fod wedi'i ysgrifennu'n wael

Mae gwraidd fy nhafod yn rhy bell i ffwrdd

Mae cartref eich genedigaeth yn angof ers amser maith

Ond ti, taid, nid ydych yn angof ynof

Mae'ch calon yn dal yn gynnes yn rhywle

Ni wnaethoch erioed ddal pwysau ceiniogau

Ond fe wnaethoch chi gynnal cyfoeth o chwerthin

A rhai geiriau o'r hen wlad

Fe ddylech chi weld y tir newydd heddiw

Mae mor aeddfed

Cartref genedigaeth newydd

Perllan deulu, ein coed, dychweliad

Ac mae'n fy atgoffa faint

Rwy'n dy garu di

(I don't know Welsh

Don't ask me to pronounce this

I know it's poorly written

The root of my tongue is too far away

The home of your birth is long forgotten

But you, Grampa, are never forgotten in me

Your heart still is warm somewhere

You never held the weight of pennies

But you held a wealth of laughs

And some words from the old land

You should see the new land today

It is so ripe

Home of new birth

Family orchard, our trees, a returning

And it reminds me how much

I love you)

BLESSING ON A SON

A wish for healthy long life and for honor
And all those pretty things
But yesterday when I followed you sprinting
Your grin spread out its wings
Flew in my praying for nothing to stop you
May running grinning sing
And may you never slow down the circus
Observing what it brings

Two days ago I observed you examine
Your head was turned aside
Collect the fortune of everything curious
Enigma's time and tide
May exploration blow sails of your searching
Amazed at mysteries wide
May knowledge become a provocative mistress
Adventure ship to ride

I bless your speedy exuberant plunging

I bless your curious quest

I pray a humble reality guide you

And put you to the test

An onward going may flow into giving

A kindly bench of rest

Your highest blessing a generous living

Do better than my best

BOLD NEWBORN

Too strong to live on others' grace
Too weak to rule the earth
Too slow to keep a city's pace
Or know what quicker living's worth

A spirit slowly infiltrates
Impregnates, giving birth
In dying downward penetrates
A broad beginning in the earth

Demands for definition are
Another face of death
A city conflagration tars
The air too far to take a breath

New dying wide beginnings breathe
A newborn into life
Old vision given from beneath
A higher cry than human flight

So if you must define the child
And we may make so bold
I'll sound naïve, or meek and mild
Denying proud belief so old

The newborn's name is "End of War"
And she will see her day
Like all the ills she killed before
She's born again to kill one more

May city rulers very well
Still bellow headlong smoke
Too loud to hear their burial bell
When from the ground new life awoke

The way the young and angry lean
They still may find some violence
But kill the tyrants' war machine
The cruel factories to silence

Bold newborn will devour the old
Traditions of the blood
She hasn't yet her method told
Her shaft now sprouting from the mud

SOFTEN

A hard night owl is destined

To own the night or die in trying

Show up in the ring for the fighting

Sacrifice the prey

Or else himself

An early bird determined

Gets the worm or else a snare

Dropping seed down here or there

Seed of breakfast sweets

Or else herself

You want to plant and grow

Something good to own

Pushing back the forest

But first in evening coolness

Soften your own ground

Know the ground is destined

To reclaim after a while

What she gave when you began

Letting you win with a smile

The final loss is not the end

DOORWAY

A thought that you like
You think it a lot
Act out on it somehow
More likely than not

An action you see
And like all the more
You claim for a habit
And open a door

A doorway unfiltered
Agnostic and wide
Both goodness and badness
Are coming inside

A room with a purpose
Is able to throw
Effects that are rotten
Out through the window

A conscience that's clean

May filter your thoughts

Refining your action

Preventing the rot

The darkest of thoughts

May find its way through

And turn out becoming

The goodness in you

A LOST SOLDIER

He may not recognize
Which way leads to home
The pictures burned into his eyes
He grapples with alone

His chariot is dragging on pavement
A wheel came off
The horse won't stop
And numbing the pain for a moment
Is all he seeks
Don't call him weak

He paid the man his share
Donated his soul
He left his pride somewhere back there
And played his bloody role

He no longer cares for the chariot

And he's not wrong

We drag along

While lifting our treasure to carry it

Along the way

To home today

He may not recognize

The point of it all

But stop and look into his eyes

And see a human soul

CHAOS AND CREATION

Broken for a moment in the dirt

I sought to understand a sudden flashing death

Grab hold on bolder life somehow

We likewise stand on icy certitude

Declare deterministic rectitude

And yet from here and now

To one millionth of a second in the future

A single mass in motion

Though taken to a trillion decimal places

Is neither fully measured in its path

Nor ever wholly forecast anywhere

Save only by itself in going

En route to melting and becoming

Along with live connecting threads

Of timeless energy that hums

No telling when or whether

Our world one day will burn

And if it gives a blaze of enemy glory

The ashes will not be the end

A fractal splitting chaos

Embedded in a blind free will

Willpower harbored both today and then

May sing tsunami songs of new creations

Be warned, testosterone froth and foam

Is not the enemy they take it for

Though whitewater time will not reverse

Revive old puppet chest-thumpers

Nor restore string pullers to a bully pulpit

Bloodthirst all gone, we take a step

To see the flame shoot up and out

Penetrating rudely as the tide

A shining seed of sunrise planted

In fields broken, soaked in death

Till a soul may finally

Learn to simply sit and listen

In the soot and charcoal

To hear creation humming from below

FREEDOM ISN'T FREE

"Freedom isn't free," they're saying
Not knowing what they mean
There will never be a shortage
Of deserts never green

Barren rocks all freed by mighty
Tornadoes of the sword
Tyrants new and gray defining
The meaning of the word

"Freedom's price is war," they're thinking
The hard will not back down
But in dreams I see a boulder
Roll down a rising ground

Berm of sand with olives growing
More free than rocky peaks
Hill of olive branches showing
An open door to peace

Gateway to long halls of shields
A flickering, gleaming view
Swords here find their idle honor
Awash in liquids new

Dip a thousand years to mix us
Old blade reshape, refine
Fit fuel to leave the cruel behind us
To feed a thirsty mind

Portal into red all blending
Blood brothers of the soil
Hardest work is gently mending
Anointing freedom in new oil

Elm or yew or eucalyptus
The woods are coming back
Into corn and soybean sadness
The roots of truth attack

Freedom isn't free; it's costing
A leap of faith away
From well-lit power into darkness
I pull my plowshare till the day

DISEMBODIED WELL

Have you ever been disembodied
And drowned in a dazzling well
Free of physical façade and fear
Leaving behind an irrelevant shell

And hovered in a water table there
A tunnel open to a dark wellspring
To look into earth's crust and hear
Infinity in between rational things

Your memory won't contain the vision
You'll never bring back the words to tell
Perhaps a snatch or tag of color
May log a voyage to watery hell

Return, stay home a physical while
You'll die and go there soon enough
The body is your house for now
Resonant waves in the well are rough

Yet disembodied visions

Showed you how to listen

To the spirit in your body

Though shedding the shell so shoddy

The ego's bullhorn sermon

Shallow and determined

Yet once or twice in a lifespan

Escape somehow while you still can

To the deep and disembodied well

To hear infinity ring her bell

OF A WORD FOR THE WISE

Of a word for the wise
And a stick for the fool
Throw it back in the pile
Or destruction will rule

There's a pile in the way
Gotta move and adjust
What you see here today
Will tomorrow be dust

Of a weight that is just
Or a measure that's even
Though we sift in the dust
We can never conceive them

What you hear with the ear
On the road will not match
But from there to back here
Separate angles you catch

Of the stacking of rocks

And of balancing fine

Piling up to treetops

Just to find out what's mine

NOBODY KNOWS

Nobody knows quite why or how

Stained chapel, a stale aroma

Holy pages, musty dust

Lid tightly screwed, and fearful now

To bottle a beast inside us

Throttling a greedy lust

Cathedral streaked in rust of chains

Pages of the book of books

Bequeath a golden prison

Caged animal claws are also stained

While sacred checks and balances

Confine a worried living

Chapel redeeming herself in light

Of sunbeams the glass reveals

Animal rising dignified

By clods of dirt on his heels

Scent of sensuous incense

Purifies a union too intense

Break the glass, a key must turn

Unleash the beast and let him learn

Flip a page to the unknown

A blank unstained creation

Bleached and dirty blond

Golden locks released

Ripple stains a holy pond

Redeem and raise a fearless beast

A game that made him once unworthy

Now a dirty holy feast

Nobody knows quite why or how

There is no explanation

A lid unscrewed, a wildness out

They breed a holier nation

End over end, head over heels

Pour out a plunging oblation

The hardest heavy crisis comes
To make for better neighbors
Of higher minds beyond the fear
Of poets and soothsayers
To skim for meaning or direction
Heads that swim in prayers

Gust and rain on church parade
The book is sopping wet
Golden clothes are see-through now
They just don't know it yet

A smile while we enjoy the view
Of soot beneath the altar
Rainforest all dynamic
Dust rinsed away, the stains are, too
A soaking dress uncovers
A life beyond their panic

Nobody knows quite why or how

It started in a chapel

Forgive our trespasses

Keys turned and lids unscrewed to flout

Commandments old and brittle

And wilder life progresses

SEEDS

Flown and blown across the globe

Roaming and collecting

Seeds and cuttings, sprigs in pots

Assorted thoughts and probes

This one laughing drunkenly

That one a sobbing ocean gale

Over here a howling glint of steel

And there a mellow glimmer

Some I watch and prune with care

Some sow hard and let go wild

The rhyme or reason I don't know

I'll learn to graft tomorrow

For today somehow these shoots

Have blown and rooted into me

I see a swaying forest in the trees

And if you feel a kindred breeze

Allow me humbly now to sow

My seed into your spirit

BOOK 3

LOOSIE GOOSIE
AND OTHER POEMS

October 2021 —
February 2022

LOOSIE GOOSIE

"Loosie goosie, frabitty dapitty doop!"

A city bum once told me,

Then eagerly gaped at my face,

Longing for a fair answer.

And too serious and tired to laugh him off,

I nodded and gazed in return

Into his bloodshot eyes and into himself

And I said, "Yes sir, that's right,"

Because it was.

And accepting my confession, he beamed a smile,

And in his yellow teeth I saw a tender humanity

Which brought me near to tears

As I felt his soul was purer than mine had ever been.

And walking on, it took me years to see

That his encounter had been for me

Poem number one.

ALIVE TODAY, POTENTIALLY

Alive today, potentially

Again tomorrow, possibly

This fragile song so dear to you

Last night was nearly done and through

The meter's crude, but not the meaning

Running rhythm cloaks a steaming

Sense of vapor doomed to fade

So insecure, the tune you made

What did it mean, the dream you had?

Why did it seem so quick and sad?

A running hard because of whom?

Till quicksand chanted early doom

The sand today is trickling

A minute hand is troubling

Your song is leaking, sing it well

Before they ring the final bell

AM I VISIBLE?

Am I visible?

Maybe still, a few lifetimes beyond my own?

Simply by virtue of writing some words?

What if being visible wasn't what I was after?

And what of the invisible ones, sisters and brothers

Each indescribably apart, sagely, aloft

Yet all joined somehow beneath the surface

Yet not all sharing our means of expression

Are they to be forever invisible?

Not while I can put a pen to paper

Hand to the heavens, each soul who allows me

Their voice I carry within my own

Absorb and transpose a sense of those

Even one or two who were silent before

Let me carry their prayer to you, each one

Beneath the surface or else above it

That another human shall never be invisible

SHOOT UP

The bang of a gun

Ejects one poem, evokes another

Hard masculine sun

Betrays a humus, assaults her cover

In choosing but one

I lose a father or lose a mother

Shoot up like a geyser, surge out with me

Leave our pains and our sins beneath

With the pains and the sins

Of souls we sprouted from

We young shoots unknowing, turn tender

Wings in lieu of roots now

Screeching through barriers, up forever

I shatter on harsh high beauties

Of electric male clouds, gleaming

Here a gentle bed of white surrounding

There a full-throated whipping fury

Our richer mother far below us

Welcoming all, seeing every child return

Molding tears into shining new lives

Holding the sins for learning

The boom of a thunder

You skip a heartbeat, I laugh aloud

We ogle in wonder

Survey a vista above the clouds

To never fly under

An all-embracing vision we found

FEATHER RUFFLED

If I ran by you in a rush

On a road to a singular future

And if in passing

I kicked your toe

Or I left a feather ruffled

Let me pause to beg your pardon

And if pardon isn't your way

And your cover is not made of feathers

Ground wasp arousing

Defend your grove

I allow a point delivered

Let me edge around the border

An improving trail may move

Not so straight are the lines of a forest

A path meanders

Disturbs a peace

So resume your law and order

While I turn my lawless corner

BACKYARD

If you aim

To cure us all

You may start

In hardened soil

Out in the yard

If you try

For nothing much

Softer earth

Cannot be matched

For silent worth

There is hope

In a reward

Fertile fields

Will have conferred

When fully healed

Lie awhile

In morning shade

Hear the flutes

Of stretching blades

And reaching roots

There is good

Atoning for

Hubris old

In giving more

Than others stole

If you wish

To leave a note

None can beat

A life rebuilt

Beneath the feet

Let it grow

Restore and rise

Give her more

Receive her prize

A better cure

COLOR BLIND

How can one who's color blind

Then hate the color red?

How can you detest a thing

You never understood?

There's a way to do it, but

I wish we lost the way

Whether for our grandchildren

Or you and me today

Drunk I write these lines of mine

To ask you what to do

Stay angry or to just accept

The way we knew is through

Analyze or just resign

Let foreign tunes resound

Allow the nature course to run

And one day come around

EVEN A DEVASTATING BEAUTY

Even a devastating beauty rejecting your advance

Aching cold of shoulder and haughty of neck

Leaves you a fertile solitude by the window

All-connecting image, proud holding up of a head

Even a seed who rots and withers away

Rather than sprouting on my time, in my sight

Enriches the tiny infinity where she lies

Slipping down to fill her mother's basket

Even a brief cup of brotherly camaraderie

Filled more with folly than higher uses

Gave an eternal sip, slurping up to the soul

Slaking a thirst for poems without words

Any word or pen stroke written, read or spoken

Will fail to strike the eternal nail's head

While with a connecting image here or there

Pops a window open, for higher uses in its time

FUNGUS SONG

1

Why and how may words convey

A living essence of wordless mechanisms

Workings carrying silent principles forward

Interweaving strands of infinite all-sweeping streams

Human hubris being what it is

And what it always was meant to be

I make myself the manner of man

Become absurd in a coarse flow of words

A horse's mouth, a grassy breath

Presuming to translate a nameless energy

Give feeble voice to almighty welling-up force

Whose language yet transcends my highest reach

Even as I lay sprawled across

Its most intimate playground

And others whose feet may play in this ground

May carry the strain in deeds or demeanor

In linking interaction, in sex beyond language

Or in painted color or musical sound

Or yet in silent, still connection

Wordless poems standing free and sensual

While I lean to a dirtier work

Of making words a coarser paintbrush

Delicately to envision

Mycelial ways of wisdom

Stroking out unevenly

What the forest invites me to paint

2

The river finds her newer course

The rhyme of which she declines to teach

Brushing by you and me

Fleeting smile at our curiosity

Absorbed only in finding and using her way

Milking it fully, licentiously

Pushing gently each twist and turn

Herding her offspring divine with herself

"Did one branch off away, alone?

It will return in time;

Visibly or invisibly, it still is mine

My love infiltrates me into them all;

The branch is me as well, yet free."

She beams, aloof to any accounting

Of three-dimensional whereabouts

How can I love so fiercely

An infinitesimal river

Or seeing her mates more fitted to my size

Or thinking of streams of universal proportions

How do I know she loves me so surely

And you so equally?

And how on earth did she find her way to me?

3

I begin to see my words as rubbish

Foreign spores arise to bow me down

Inspire my hand to cover my mouth

All purposes are way out there

Unreachable beyond the farthest unseen

And what can I know of intentions?

After nine blows beating, a tenth attempt

Punching at I know not what or where

Hot air begets a mildew scent

There went the empty lines

More correctly, this song can only be written

After at least a year's vow of silence

Sweating and alternatively sitting still

On the topsoil like an animal

A year I pray to take one day

And yet for now, impatient blood overcomes

And plays its ready note, bursting from my veins

Beginning the poem of poems

Early and rough, pulsating

Early and rough as the ending of

The lives of the best of men

4

Legacy is nothing, opportunity is all

Openings to flow and fill with life

Bringing in its living wake the eternal glow

Of sweet and swallowing blue death

And thick and black continues the flow

Rivulets bend a bubbly path

Through a tangle of undergrowth

Pain and anguish mingling

Adding heat and spice and tang

Sharp rocky shoals pour in their own

Salt into an open wound

She winds along, around and through

The easiest way to patiently heal

Multiplying and transforming all

Refusing not a one, yet along the way

Some she deposits earlier than others

Foaming surge to smiling meander

She fits and forms to shape the time

Soaking up each rhythm offered along her course

Confining her own song to not a single demand

Though entering each, and making to be entered

But the sliding beat of her march

Few can keep up with

Watching helplessly her form and passion

As she slips on and off each bond of holding

To the tune of an invisible will

5

A silence may correct the meaning

And how it makes us feel is irrelevant

For if you decide the flow is wicked

To you it becomes the depths of hell

While those withholding judgement

She sweeps along in every good direction

Whether perceived or not

Most fortunate of all the moist eye

Which pauses to dwell on her beauties

And gratefully view

The way she penetrates all with her flow

And is penetrated with all reality's thrusts

Assimilating all into her symphony

The physical into the spiritual

And on into new creations

6

The immortal river tends toward

What she already has made inevitable

While she hums to me in sweet and fluid notes

That she tends toward something true

And something better than we know

And better than we are

And toward something we will be made part of

Only in the crudest way can this emission

Be called a poem, technical, traditional

Call it and me what you will

And call it crude and ugly and rude

Yet know that a real mycelial flow

Lightly snickers at plain technicality

And recycles each tradition in its time

Accompanied by the rich aromas of a swamp

7

Relinquishing, surrendering, open everything

If only a chosen place and time

Allow a throbbing heart to ache

At the unspeakable, untouchable, enormous

Magnificence of her eternal flow

She blasted through my heart and on to yours

The piercing was not an ending

But rather a new opening

A closing loop flipping to a new one in spirals

Any fungus song appears as drivel

If you push to rationally analyze her

Yet regardless of all she carries through

The key to life and goodness

8

And just when you thought the last note hummed

Spurting through an unknown gap

Comes a fresh flow, familiar yet brand new

Injecting itself sweetly, pungently, insistently

Into a certain wrinkle of the mind

For working miracles on a parallel plane

Shadow dimensions of foreign familiarity

Unsettled, never done, unstable, never gone away

She is everywhere you look

Even when you perceive not a bit of her

She is your very eyesight, the essence of it

Not separate from or above you or me

Not only in us, but throughout our being

And all being we connect with forever

9

Finally comes a time

To push beyond a straight-edged quest

For any full consensus

To swirl beneath, around, over, through

Any obstacle presented

Making time her dearest friend and ally

The rhythm of the song is unrecognized

And will forever remain so

As it forever remains new and untested

Vibrant and defiant, even in the silence

Nothing ever was more brimming full

With beauty and passion

Nor likewise with stoic resolve, untouchable

Unattainable, she is already attained

LOOKING DOWN

If I tapped in and connected

To you in one of these my lines

Brought about a living peace of wild mind

Yet never look up to me

As if, all-knowing, I plucked the words

From where they rested in my own hardware

No, look down

Every true connection came from the deep

Reached out to me from the living soil

Passage to a new earth in the old dirt

Look to her

And to your beautiful naked toes digging into her

The flesh and sensual linking to her

You may find a higher piece of mind than mine

By looking down

CARBON AND WATER

Shut up about gold and silver

There burns the almighty dollar

The intangible may get farther

But listen to carbon and water

Smoky male and female fluid

Seeking each a returning down

Soiling, soaking, come renew it

Sink, redeem a reviving ground

Binary coin of life organic

Before the earliest barley field

Biology above the market

Beneath the rebel who made the wheel

The economy breaks down in my lines

Distracting, my trees sing to me of woody mulch

And streams or ponds or drizzle days

My pockets yearn to be empty of any token

Save a pair of pruners

Or better yet a pocketful of olives

How can I put a price on these perfections?

Made like every other fruit, like you and me

Out of our mother's currency

Carbon and water

ROUNDABOUT THE EAGLE FLYING

Roundabout the eagle flying

Clouds of thunder, clouds of war

Till beyond the storm now gliding

Bursting from the clouds, we soar

Higher rising

Higher rising

Peaks we never flew before

Peaks we never flew before

Mountain peaks behind and forward

Scold and taunt and beckon me

Strike a chord and drum a rhythm

Deep and surging, wild and free

Eagle flying

Eagle flying

Look, my neighbor, can you see?

Look, my neighbor, can you see?

When below I see that river

Laughing will I take my dive

Knowing there the deadly current

Flows as free as eagles fly

Free forever

Free forever

You and I one day will be

You and I one day will be

DID YOU THINK

Did you think this book would be like

An uneventful jaunt, an easy forest?

A rhyming pretty stroll in loblolly pines?

Don't trip now on this boulder,

A brash outcropping or a firmer footing,

A pad for stepping off into rebellion.

Did you think my land, my people,

The whole American people,

Have passed our prime or forfeited the future

Simply by a capital's scheming institutions

Losing control of an empire?

Did you think our flame was waning?

Did you think our fiery spirit

Should burn itself to death in guilt or shame

Examining our bloody hands or dirty deeds?

Did you think a silent darkness was an answer

To a light that shone too clumsily or dim

Where no light before had entered?

Did you think mankind would find now

Other truths, still more self-evident

Than the bedrocks of my nation's soul?

Did you think you'd find salvation

In rising to oppose our earthy clans

Who never cease to rise above ourselves?

Did you think that for one moment

Your pessimistic march would hold a candle

To the brilliant dawn we even now are planting

In all the rocky soil you thought was dead?

If you had these nonsense inklings, friend,

Sit a while, rest your feet, and think again.

TO LIE AWAKE

To lie awake on a mattress

Turn to face home, then turn away

Stare into night, silence droning persistent

Tapping, tapping on the skull

Silent as stone

Oh, to lie asleep again on cold hard ground

Humming along a cicada cadence

A rougher mattress symphony

Forgetting this silence that taps tonight

That cracks the stone at last

Something somehow

Flowing out now

Somewhere a window blowing open

A cricket hops in on the wind

To lie awake and play his solo

He learned on a twig and topsoil mattress

When he was at home

CAN'T PULL MY EYES OFF THE SIGHT

Can't pull my eyes off the sight

Of licking flames, mesmerizing

Up in smoke I see them going

Half the assumptions of yesterday, vanished

Half the knowledge prized by grandfathers

While a grandmother's intuition lies immune

Remaining intact like a hidden stone

Even if cracked and reimagined

To the quieter truths of religion I bow my head

Grateful to friends who hold them safe

While a masculine deity of flaming jealousy

I see going relegated to his rightful place

In a pantheon with humbler gods together

Older and younger labor as one

In concert playing after millennia apart

To the beat of an almost feminine rhythm

I can nearly see the symphony now

Hovering a moment on the edges of my reality

But I can't pull my eyes off the sight

TREE ALIVE

Tree alive

A knowledge fresh

A bitter flavor

In the flesh

Four alive

One man, one wife

One tree of knowledge

One of life

Three alive

A naked game

A crooked diamond

Digging shame

Live the dream

Taste Eden shades

Of gods and serpents

Kings and knaves

See the prize

A hiss you hear

And swiftly cover

Eyes and ears

Quick rewind

Play back the scene

Win back the garden

Lose the game

To defy

And curious go

Obeying never

Seek to know

What it means

You'll never see

Till dreams or dying

Make you free

LEMON JUICE

Stand by a tangy kitchen window in body

Lemon juice spilled in a slice, a crack

A crevasse of cut months, then of years

Gone, dripping down, never to get back

Anger, the sour sting slowly fades

Sweeter aftertaste remains in the pores

The time was not a full and smarting loss

Its spirit brought you here to stand

Yellow sunrays extend in the window

A GLASS RAISED HERE

To a word not spoken

When the absence played a perfect part

To a loud explosion

Where the shrapnel found a worthy mark

To a bolt of lightning

Striking down a tree already dead

To a scowl frightening

From a god whose book was never read

To the good and evil

Holding lies and truth and roles to play

To unanswered riddles

Never heard or seen in light of day

To a past unwinding

Every twist and turn along a path

To a gradual climbing

To a higher science, higher math

To a soul upgrading

Falling silent here to wake up there

Eyes no longer waiting

Not a sight rejecting, lighter air

To a full believing

All-encompassing and piercing free

To a spear-tip rising

Lying ready inside you and me

To a deed of legend

Where an action spoke a million lines

To the world we live in

There's a glass raised here for all of time

IT

This is it, the ultimate one
The passing scent of lentil stew is it
Extraction of life's savory satisfactions
All else falls away, for better or worse
This moment is become all

This is it, the ultimate one
Fresh leaves of mint I crush between my thumbs
To dip my tongue and hold it in my teeth now
All else falls away, the day is renewed
This moment is a page turned

This is it, the ultimate one
My own—myself—become irrelevant
I see and hear a climax of a woman
All else falls away, the night is reborn
She now is my religion

This is it, the ultimate one

Red Edom is a ghost I carry on

A feel of scarlet struggle through the senses

All else falls away, for better in time

This moment is become it

THE DIVE AND THE RIPPLES

In my thirty-seventh year a dive began

The ripples I guessed and contemplated

Eternal tensions roll between

One side of a splash and the other

One's own side and the far side, inscrutable

The dive and the ripples

Bringing a task to completion

Being prime mover, an instigator

Or else in ascending, outsource the labor

Play a note to its final breath

Not hearing yet the symphony it joins

Into whose sound its ripples mingle

Sing the eternal tension between

The dive and the ripples

A house repaired, a home renewed

A venture commenced, building raised

Vision seized, hot and reckless dive into it

Seed planted, land embraced, eye opened

A thing born, image presented, note carried through

Deity appeased, aroused, a woman satisfied

Hands then release, let fly free, each ripple to its way

This splash will last for years between

The dive and the ripples

Your own act, your sacred inner impetus

Relinquish every sluggish hesitation

All may be determined from beyond you, yet

There is not a single real limitation on you

Your plunge will be your own, not mine nor God's

A splash of unmatched beauty in your time

And let eternal tension play her tune between

The dive and the ripples

SELF-EVIDENT

Self-evident, pulsing, in the morning you run

Three old colors race up a flagpole

Not for the suits walking in stone buildings

Not for the lanes that would bind us in tight

Run loose for the blood that binds our tribes together

Blood blending, soaking us into each other

Harming each other, freeing each other

Shattering shackles of tyrants in anger

Pursuing a prize, a future of honor

Heroes, known or nameless, run the invisible track

Each drop from the veins of each one, self-evident

Against the world, for life, for liberty, for pursuit

For giving a life for one's friends of all colors

Self-evident, pulsing, immortal they run forever

In their morning shadow we run along

Our colors, our eyes, our pulse, our same old truth

Carrying our bond, each divine, each self-evident

PAX LIBER

I searched far and wide in cool forest air

For a central head, a ruler ejaculating doctrines

Laying divine dogmas down for the rest

A prototype I hoped for an imagined peace on earth

In terra pax hominibus

But there I found no brutish subjugation to compare

To pax romanas of older memories

Nor to any pax americana more benign

(Though clumsy, she one day will come alive)

And I wondered how we never yet have seen

A pax christiana to vindicate all the hot air

Then finally I resigned to sitting mute in the woods

Like a silent brute in the dirt

Accepting there a pax liber

BURY ALL THE BLOODY HATCHETS

Bury all the bloody hatchets

Encase the lot in stone

There descendants' graveyard lesson

Of bad old days forever gone

Show the broken chains and shackles

Do not forget the pain

Go and know the story follows

Again it comes, but not the same

Chopping down each other's towers

Amused for several days

Grew a grip of muscled power

To find more worthy heights to raze

Lay the wreaths for bloody heroes

Pay the men their due

Say they stood and never wavered

Performing all they knew to do

Take the tools the heroes gave us

Grip and make our stand

Dig the hatchets' grave yet wider

The blood on them will heal the land

UNDERLYING BITE

Under the crunch of a tooth in a fruit

A real relation slips

Fluid eluded ten thousands of years

Quietly finally drips

Rife with the flavor of separate sprays

Inviting ruby mist

Spiked are the drops, hidden juice slurping up

Spike hammered down in my wrist

One hand is holding debauchery wild

The other a holly stake

Skewer a fruit and relinquish a child

Sharp is the bite you will take

Seizing a bite of becoming apart

No longer part of One

Raising my tower to tackle the stars

Syllables coming undone

Ripe was the gift of a gardener doomed

A woman's fresh red smile

Crunchy a section of separate pods

Seizing my gaze for a while

Chewing a mystery timeless and dark

Of plucking with a hand

Nailing it down on the splinters and bark

Giving or taking unplanned

Mouthful of seeds I may spew on the ground

Red pools below my feet

Breathing in agony, stretching apart

Paradise mingles beneath

Split my experience away from the soul

Ten thousand years or so

Spike them and hammer together the whole

Biting, inviting to know

Never to grip the Objective of love

Forever know a bond

Ceasing a grasping forever above

Slurp what is hidden beyond

Looser and easier fruits will be had

In depth instead of height

Fleshy or crunchy or bitter or sweet

Closing your eyes while you bite

Helper was helping me reach up to see

To think, therefor to be

Climbing to think I created myself

Falling from everything free

Munching enigma, cohesion intrudes

It's sticky in the teeth

Crimson and drippy and trippy and sharp

Under a gnawing beneath

FAR OUT

Far out on a wavering limb

To teeter on a slippery brink

Edge of precipitous silence humming

Periphery of huddling crowds in the wind

Head down, eyes forward

Hard stride in a blinding blizzard

Out from the pious camp

Campfires fade in a pitch-black swamp

Precariously planting the feet

Curiously balanced and braced

Feel my way till the last breath leaves

Find the last lonesome clue

Here is the still small voice

Here a yawning gulf of wonder

Here heavenly patterns on frozen surfaces

Here may be found I know not what

To extend beyond the boundaries

To follow divergent ways far away

To recklessly feast the eyes, set apart

To bring a partner as an afterthought

The fall-outs who wouldn't keep up

The cautious who stayed in the group

For their sakes I leave them alone

Their salvation I find far out in a storm

Hands out as I tiptoe, holding the void

One hand holding a clump of soil

The other a bleeding, weeping, dreaming pen

Step along and balance

Far out on a limb

BRIGHTER FAITH

The smell of the woods is spellbinding

While telling a story unsure

The health of the spirit is building

Unwinding a yarn of before

The wealth of the heathen is gathered

Enlarging a stewardship pure

Toward a green light we are climbing

Envision devotion more bright

A lighter more open-eyed finding

A flying by faith and by sight

While older men scold and admonish

Still stuck in the wrong and the right

BRACE

Brace

Brace

Brace yourself

Here they come

Stop the drum

Come dig in tight, come stand as one

Brace

Brace

Brace yourself

Here's the day

Men will say

They came to take our home away

Give 'em hell

Rebel yell

Come plant the flag and ring that bell

Brace

Brace

Brace yourself

Never kneel

Plant your heel

Achilles' spirit, blade of steel

Strike the head

Adam's dead

Arising sons, we break the bread

Spill the wine

Now's the time

We make them pay a bloody fine

Brace

Brace

Brace yourself

Later on

Haters gone

Resume the beat

The peaceful song

SOMETHING

Did I trumpet loud the virile impetus?

Or stir up a stoic path of force?

Did I slurp in every pleasure known?

Throw a hip outside a comfort zone?

Let it be a step, a facing up to something.

Did I push into a muddy unknown den?

Wade and plumb the depths of shallow men?

Did I seize your girl or offer mine?

Undermine foundations cased in time?

Let it be a plunge, a diving down to something.

Did I sing a dream of peace on earth?

Did I mourn a death and cheer a birth?

Did I praise a sunrise, gaze at blood?

Did I burst a dam, unleash a flood?

Let it be a stab, a piercing into something.

Did I fully feel how little may be traced

Of the energy and matter, time and space?

Did I sense how truer yet what lies outside?

Did I lose myself to hear a boundless tide?

Let it be a trip, a journey out to something.

Let the unbelievers slowly climb each rung

Let believers thump a book and wag a tongue

Let the scientific method press along

Let the impulse of the masses cycle on

Let me eat, drink, work, and give my thanks to
     Something.

NAKED

Naked was I occasionally born

And the light of liberty was in the eye

When with the naked eye I saw a living light

Your life blossomed in my open eye

Before returning to dust yet naked

Forever past and future

Then the third day I got up and dressed

As I heard a body's supposed to do

Receiving gifts of shame and skin of sacrifice

A new cover they called "liberty"

A new collecting, they called it "justice"

They gather past with future

Naked the dawn of numberless days

A beginning uttering, a word with God

The time is gone to gather; scatter now abroad

A truth blossoms in a nakedness

A timeless learning to love thy neighbor

Forever past and future

A BOLT OF LIGHTNING

A bolt of lightning I bring to you

Blue skies were long forgotten

A heavy cover of clouds you knew

The weight of ages on them

A generation awaited long

Old picture in the ocean

A son of thunder, a son of song

The sky is cracking open

To split the air and divide the time

A slicing in the fabric

To spear a cloud and forever climb

Though burning, never frantic

I'm looking down in a jarring jolt

A power quick and sudden

Though hard and heavy, my lightning bolt

May not become a burden

THE PROSAIC TURN

Bright lightning cracks in a loving night

A dazzling sight, and tightly might you hold it

Scattering eternal questions on the surface

Dim flickering vision, a flashing of heaven

Still feeling untouched by simple transmission

Till flash to bang no longer is delayed

Now sunny thunder in his turn

Drops an anchor

Smacks away the subtle vision

Illuminated brighter, logical, longer

Stronger the sound than was the sight

And who in turn may finally deny

Loud sunlight is better than flickering darkness?

Only from a place of anchored boldness

May fuller dreams shoot free of anchors

And only greenhouses built of reason

Bring love to blossom in liveliest color

And the highest flights of trance may not compare

To beautiful dirt on the blue of a worker's collar

The banal and trivial elbow jostle

The salty sand and rougher noisy gravel

Shortsightedness of menial attentions

A simple focused mind under the sun

Others tinkering with institutions

Others' muscle and the sweat outshining all

Each of these can shine between the lines

Where poems worth their salt will open up

And still a flickering throbbing mystery

A tribal song may rise in turn

May crack perception's egg at night

The black beneath your eyelid hums a tune

Which may not be denied if you are true

And tightly may you hold

Dark longings from of old

While in the day you gather stones

To build prosaic walls of cities strong

Of taller, louder binding songs

To roughly answer agitated questions

Unanswerable when scattered in our dreams

Now a time has come to be awake

I had my clumsy turn; now you create